TEEN · GUII

MARRIED LIFE

Liz Friedrich

20P

Franklin Watts

London · New York · Toronto · Sydney

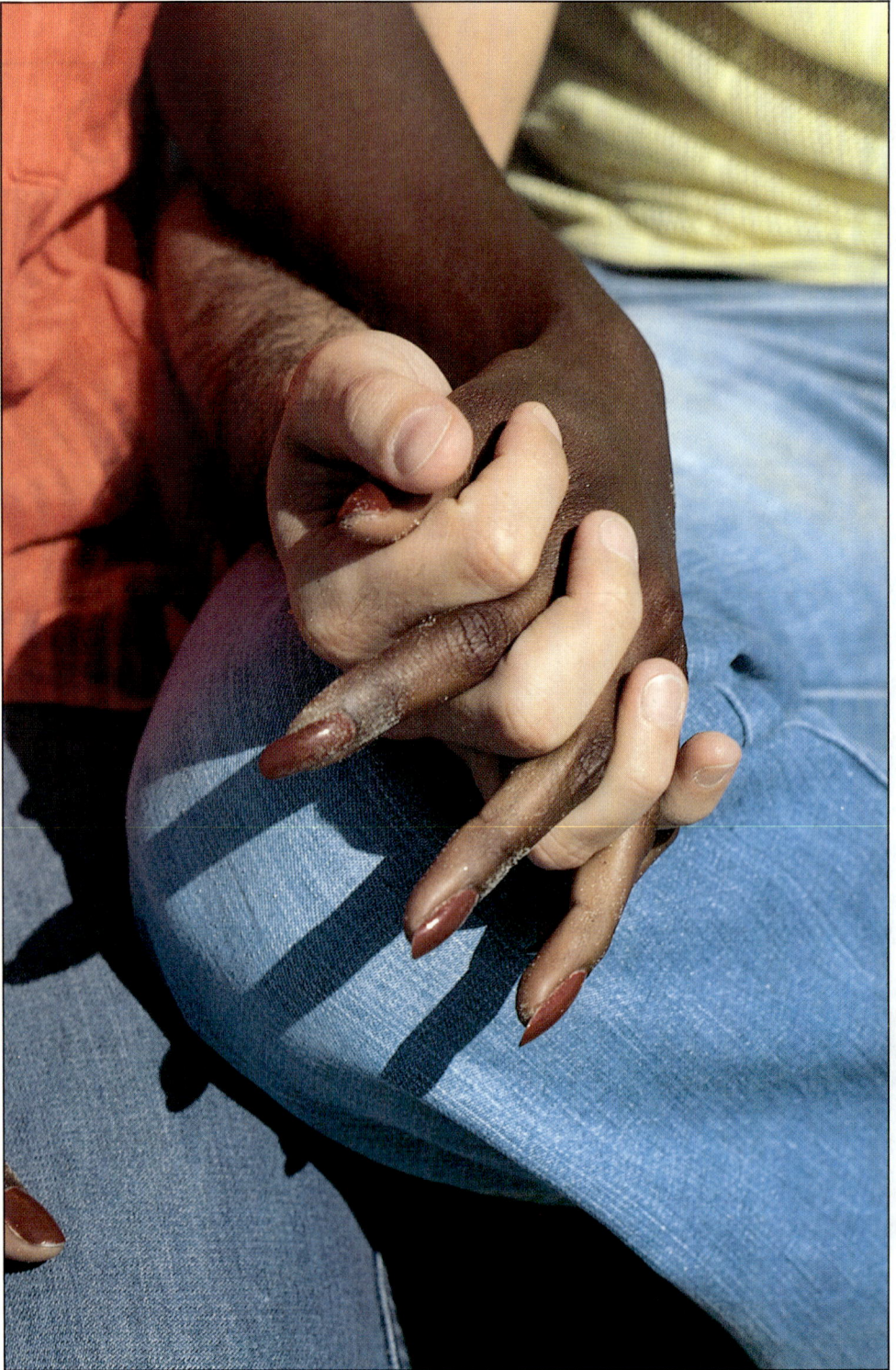

Chapter One:
Choosing the Right Partner

Side by side, hand in hand... But are they sure it's really love? Can they be certain they are right for each other? Will it last?

You are in love, and thinking about marriage. How do know if this is the right person for you?

Falling in love

Falling in love is a magical and exciting experience, so much so that sometimes we are just in love with love:

"I first fell in love when I was 16. What I remember most about it wasn't really the girl herself but how I felt. It was all this romantic yearning. I used to write songs about her and sit in my room for hours playing my guitar and singing."

Knowing that a person is right for you is, in the last resort, a *"gut"* feeling. And the right marriage partner is not necessarily the first person we fall in love with. This story is typical:

Meeting at a party.

"*I fell passionately in love when I was still at school. We saw each other almost every day, and when we didn't meet we wrote each other long letters. We talked vaguely about marriage a few times but I think I always felt deep down that something so intense couldn't last – and it didn't.*"

That is the problem with falling in love, you can also fall out again.

Falling in love is sometimes described as a kind of madness. It can certainly have severe symptoms: lack of appetite, not sleeping, absentmindedness, obsession with another person. If we didn't call it love we might send the afflicted person off to the doctor. In this "*deranged*" state it is not surprising that our judgement can be severely affected. "*Love is blind*" a cliché, but all too true.

"*I was always falling in love and they always seemed wonderful at first. But after a while they turned out to be bastards! Until I met Charlie, that is. Perhaps I've grown up. He was very different. I came to love him gradually as I got to know him better.*"

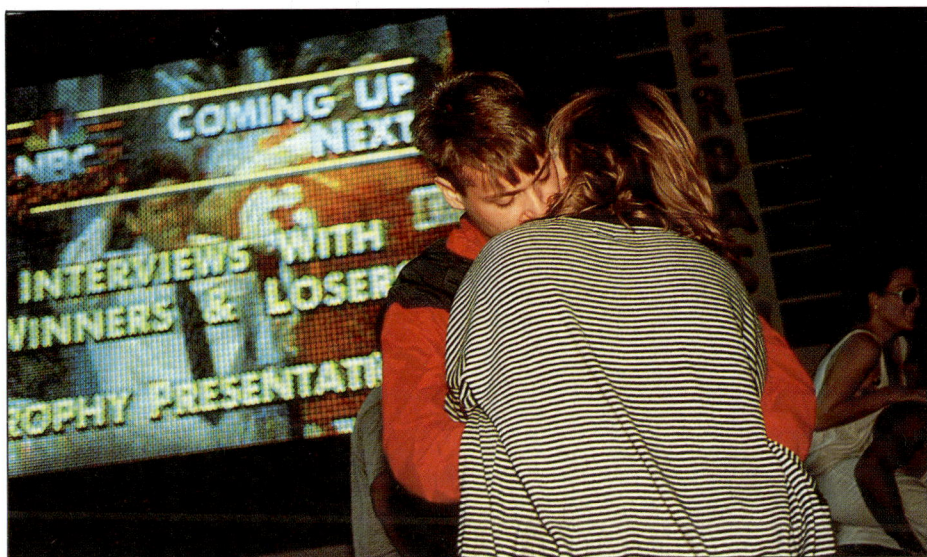

Falling in love.

The real thing

Does being in love always lead to marriage? Do you have to be in love for marriage to work? Everyone hopes for a lasting relationship when they marry. Such a **relationship** has to be based on loving someone, not just on "*being in love with love*".

Loving someone is romantic. But it is not about seeing them through "*rose-coloured glasses*". It means accepting them and the possibility that there will be problems. It means caring about someone, respecting them, feeling at ease and sharing a sense of humour. Feeling "*right*" together and wanting to share your life with someone. It is the single most important reason for getting married.

The right reasons ?

Falling in love is not something you choose to do – it just happens. But getting married *is* a choice, probably the most important one in your life.

Getting married is a major decision.

You may be drifting through school, going to college to please your parents, uncertain of the kind of job you want. But the decision to marry is for you and you alone to make. There may be many factors involved in your decision. It makes sense to look at your reasons for deciding to get married and ask yourself if they are sound ones.

There is no set of "*right*" reasons. But there are some reasons which are clearly better than others, and some which are unlikely to lead to a successful marriage. For instance:

"*I can rescue him from **alcoholism** or her from drugs.*"

You cannot make anyone change. If you can't live with someone as they are, then don't marry them.

"*Some of my friends are married – what if I miss my chance?*"

This is a very common feeling called "*peer pressure*". But it's not a good enough reason to get married.

"*I want a regular sex life / My partner is incredibly attractive / We have an amazing sexual relationship."*

Sex is an important part of marriage, but it's not the most important part. If for some reason you could not have a sexual relationship, would you still want to be with this person?

"I want a baby."

Is it fair to marry just to provide a parent for *"your"* baby? How long would the relationship last?

"I want to be independent, escape from my parents, have a home of my own. Being married would make me feel adult."

This is about growing up and taking responsibility for yourself. You need to be your own person before you can share your life with someone else.

The right time

"I feel ready for a long term relationship, I'd like to share my life with someone."

"I'm ready to bring up a family."

These are feelings that grow with maturity. You begin to look at relationships differently.

Possible problems

The success of a marriage doesn't just depend on you and your partner. We are all part of society and are affected by it. However strongly you believe that *"love conquers all"*, there are situations which could obviously create problems. You would be foolish not to think carefully and ask yourselves some tough questions before marrying in these circumstances.

A big difference in age

Jane is 16, Howard is 40. Paul is 17, Sheila is 35. The age difference may not seem to matter now, but how about in 20 years time? Are these

How significant is the age difference?

couples quite sure they want a marriage partner – or are they wanting a parent-child relationship?

Differences in social background

Susan's dad is a university lecturer, her mum a solicitor. Dean's dad is a lorry driver, his mum a school dinner lady. Are there situations in which he feels defensive about his family, or she feels apologetic about hers?

Different racial or cultural background

Ama's family are black and from Ghana, Dawn's parents are white West Country farmers. Can they cope with the **racism** they will undoubtedly encounter, possibly even in their own families? Karl's German mother is a housewife, and proud of it. Jane plans a career in the bank. Are Karl and Jane clear how they each see a wife's role?

Racial or cultural differences can pose difficulties.

Differences in religion

Ruth is from a Jewish family, Dave is a non-practising Catholic. If their religion is important to them, the difficult issues will be obvious. Even if they no longer practice their religion, attitudes are deep-rooted and family pressures can be powerful, especially when it comes to bringing up children.

Both partners still in their teens

John is 19 years old and working in a warehouse, but he has been unemployed. Marcia is 17 and plans to do a course in computing at the local college. Both live at home.

Marcia will make new friends at college, she may develop new interests. Will John feel left out? How will they manage financially especially if John becomes unemployed again? Where will they live, can they afford somewhere of their own?

Family matters

It is not just the deliberate choices we make which influence our choice of partner.

"*I'm marrying you, not your family*" is often a cry from the heart. However, families are the most important influence in shaping our attitudes and ideas. Even when we think we are very different, family attitudes have a surprising way of surfacing when we are under pressure. Getting to know your partner's immediate family and introducing him or her into your own will tell each of you a lot more about the other.

Families often condition our choice of partner. Not just because they approve or disapprove of the friends we bring home, but also in determining who we find attractive.

Attraction is a complex physical and **psychological** process. Our very first experience of love and security is with our parents or a parent figure. When we are older and meet someone who reminds us of our parent, we

Family opinions often influence a relationship.

are naturally attracted to them. Sadly, this is also true when we have had bad experiences.

History often repeats itself in a family. Girls from violent homes may marry men who end up beating them. Men with cold, distant mothers may choose to marry cold, distant girls. The situations may not be happy ones but they seem safe because they are familiar. Or we may deliberately seek out someone very different in an attempt not to repeat the experience. Either way, our past experience shapes our choice. Brothers and sisters are important too. Again we may tend to repeat relationships: a bossy older sister may marry a **dependent** "*younger brother*".

The perfect fit

Another unconscious influence on how we choose a partner is the need for someone who "*fits*" with our own personality. We may choose a partner who supplies the characteristics we lack : a quiet, shy person marries someone talkative and out-going; an anxious, uncertain person marries someone confident and controlling. This often works well, but couples can become very dependent on one another. One partner may feel they have to be ambitious or anxious for both. As a result, the other partner never gets a chance to develop.

On the other hand, we may choose someone just like ourselves. This helps us to feel more confident and boosts our self-image. Things can also get difficult when either person becomes easily angry, tends to get depressed or lacks confidence.

Chapter Two:
Why
Marriage?

*They've been going
together for quite a while.
They have a lot of fun. He
has a flat and she's
thinking of moving in with
him. So who needs
marriage?*

When questioned, most young people say they expect to get married. Yet the media are always telling us that marriage is under threat and moral standards are in decline. Is marriage in decline? Is it an out-dated institution ? Why marry at all?

Living together

"We really love each other. We don't need a piece of paper to keep us together. We don't want to be tied to one another legally."

One of the differences between living together and being married is a legal one. Married partners have legal rights and obligations. This is particularly important if the marriage ends in divorce, especially for a woman. The law recognises her right to equal shares of the couple's home and money. If a couple who have been "living together" separate the woman will not be entitled to anything except some support for their children. She may have helped to furnish a home, may have cooked and washed and ironed, brought up their children and given up her job. But she can be left with no home, no money and not much chance of a job. In these days of **"sexual equality"** she will have allowed herself to become dependent and helpless.

The other important difference between living together and marrying is

Living together can be very different to marriage.

16

that living together is a very private affair. There is no public commitment to one another, no pressure to stay together. While you are young this may be an **asset**. As you get older you may feel that you want to make a public commitment to a relationship and to the effort that it can take to make it work, despite difficulties.

Some people talk about living together as being a kind of rehearsal for marriage. But it seems that the two are very different. There is no evidence that people who have lived together have more stable marriages. If anything, the reverse is true. It is people with strong religious and moral beliefs who are least likely to divorce and also are the least likely to live together first.

Changes in marriage patterns

There have been a lot of changes in the pattern of marriage during the last few decades.

People are now marrying at an older age than they were 20 years ago. The average age is now 25 for women and 26 for men. There are fewer pressures on people to marry young: it is not necessary to marry to have a sexual relationship and it is more socially acceptable than ever before for people to live together.

Pregnancy is no longer seen as a reason for getting married. As recently as 30 years ago, if a girl became pregnant the only acceptable solution was marriage, even if it meant a so-called "*shot-gun wedding*" with the reluctant groom chased up the aisle by an angry father-in-law. Today **abortion** is fairly readily available and there is little shame in being a single mother.

There have been many changes in women's lives during this century. This has had a great effect on marriage. Women may not yet have achieved full equality with men but they have better opportunites in education and jobs than ever before. Today the debate is about the problem for women of combining job and family. A woman without children can earn a reasonable living. She no longer has to be dependent on a man for her income.

Despite these changes, marriage has never been more popular. More than 90 per cent of the population in Britain and the United States will be married at some time in their lives. Even in Sweden, where many couples live together with virtually the same **legal rights** as a married couple and may have one or two children, most eventually marry.

The need of humans to get together in pairs seems to be a deep one and is found all around the world. Human infants are totally helpless and remain dependent for a long time on their mothers. A partner helps to provide support and care while she is pregnant and nursing the infant. Psychologically, we seem to have a need to recreate the comfort and security of our first relationship with our parents. However exciting new

Different cultures have different traditions.

relationships may be, most adults eventually want the stability and security of a long-term relationship. Parents often see their task as incomplete until their children "*settle down*" into marriages.

Marriage has survived all kinds of social change. In the West we see it as a romantic union where partners choose one another on the basis of love. This idea is one that has developed over the past few hundred years. Marriage used to have a far more practical basis. It was arranged between two families and was less about love than property, the ability of a man to provide for a family and the ability of a woman to produce children. In country areas, couples did not usually marry until the girl was pregnant.

Arranged marriages

There are still many societies where arranged marriages are the **norm**: Asian, Greek, Turkish, Jewish. In countries such as Kenya, Japan, Italy and Ireland families still play a very significant role in deciding who will marry

An Asian marriage.

whom.

In a society where marriage is arranged, young people are very carefully **chaperoned**. Young women will have little opportunity to get to know anyone of the opposite sex. Although the young people themselves will usually have the final say in the choice of a marriage partner, the relationship between the two families is just as important. Everyone expects that **wooing** and love come after the wedding rather than before it. Frequently they do. Where both partners give their whole-hearted consent to the marriage, it is successful.

In many traditional societies there is a growing pressure for more freedom for young people to choose their own partners.

Increased divorce

In the West marriage seems to be becoming less stable. One third of all marriages in Britain and the United States end in divorce. Though many of those who divorce re-marry, second and third marriages have an even higher divorce rate.

There are many explanations put forward for the increase in the divorce rate. Some people believe that divorce has become too available so that couples give up too easily in trying to solve their problems. Others blame the relaxed attitude of so many people to sex outside marriage. Another explanation is that easier divorce has simply revealed the true levels of unhappiness and allowed people to escape from intolerable situations. Higher expectations of marriage and the greater independence of women are undoubtedly also important.

Another important factor may be that marriage has never been expected to last as long as it is today. People now live much longer than they did 100 years ago. In the 16th century the average length of a marriage was 17 years, when it would be ended by the death of one of the partners. Today to be together *"until death us do part"* can mean 40 to 50 years of marriage.

For a particular couple, marriage can fail for many reasons. It can be because of personal difficulties – maybe the couple were never really suited. Or it could be problems such as unemployment, money difficulties, no proper home. If you are having problems in your relationship, it is easier to solve them if you are not worrying about whether you can pay the rent.

It is these kind of problems that make teenage marriages the most likely to end in divorce. Teenagers seldom earn enough to be able to afford to live away from home, some will be trying to manage on a student grant. Often this means a young couple have to live with parents which is seldom easy. Finding a job can also be a problem.

The other difficulty faced by teenagers is that most of us do a lot of growing-up in our late teens. We are still in the process of becoming independent of our parents, and forming our own opinions.

Divorce can be a painful experience.

Chapter Three:
Getting Married

The idea of a wedding may be a romantic one, but the reality involves a lot of careful planning. Are you ready for such a step?

You have weighed up the **pros and cons**. You are in love, certain you are right for each other, and you have decided to get married. For some people the next obvious and immediate step is to get married as soon as possible. But most people prefer to become engaged first.

Becoming engaged

An engagement gives you time to plan and talk together about the future, a time to check that you are making the right decision and, if necessary, change your mind. You are bound to have some doubts and uncertainties. Getting engaged will be exciting and fun, a time for good wishes and congratulations, but, like any change in our lives, it is also stressful and will have a negative as well as a positive aspect.

You may find yourself wondering: *Do I really want to give up my freedom, am I ready to settle down? How can I be certain I have made the right choice*? There may be moments when you look at your fiancée, who has seemed so wonderful until now and think, "*Surely this can't be the person I'm going to marry*".

Talking to your fiancée or a close friend whose judgement you trust will help you decide if your doubts are justifed. It is important to talk honestly about your feelings, even if you're afraid of hurting your fiancée.

Doubts can affect any relationship.

Hopefully both your families will be pleased for you. Unfortunately this isn't always the case. Parents may feel: *"He's not good enough for my daughter"*; *"She's too young to get married"*; *"I'm not ready to be someone's mother-in law, or a grandmother"*; *"I'm losing my baby"*.

If parents seem very critical it may well disguise these kinds of feelings. You are making changes in their lives as well as your own. They may also feel conscious of the contrast between your new and exciting relationship and their own. One of the benefits of an engagement is that it gives everyone time to adjust.

The Wedding

When it comes to planning the wedding, there are any number of books and magazines to tell you all about the practical aspects. There is a whole industry devoted to getting married and to persuading you to spend money on your wedding.

A wedding is still a very important **ritual** in our society. It marks an important change in your life. Most couples still choose to get married in church. Many of those who choose a registry office still want to make it a formal occasion. Over 70 per cent of couples have a white wedding.

Societies all around the world celebrate a wedding with rituals to encourage **fertility**, happiness and good fortune. These can last for several days. In the West the religious ceremony is usually fairly brief and attention tends to centre just as much on the celebrations that follow.

Traditionally it is the bride's family that pays most of the cost of the wedding and the cost of a white wedding and reception is likely to be several thousand pounds. A couple needs to decide just what kind of wedding they want and their families can afford. They should be careful to make sure that the costs of the special occasion do not get in the way of making a new home.

A traditional white wedding.

If your ideas about the wedding match up with those of your parents, well and good, but what if the bride's mother has always dreamt of her daughter floating up the aisle in yards of lace, while the couple themselves had envisaged a small gathering at the registry office? Ultimately it is your wedding and your own choice. Your parents or in-laws may not agree with many other things that you decide in the course of your marriage, but making your own decisions, even if they prove to be mistakes, is part of establishing yourselves as a couple. This does not mean that you cannot be tactful and respect the fact that parents may have some very strong feelings about what they believe to be right. There is usually some kind of compromise to be reached about who will be invited and to what kind of celebration.

As the big day approaches, often the doubts do too. It is easy to feel that you are being taken over by the process especially if you are having a big, formal wedding with lots of guests and presents. You may feel that you could not call off the wedding even if you wanted to. This in itself can become a source of tension and lead to quarrels.

"About a week before the wedding I got really depressed. Everyone seemed to talk about nothing but weddings. I began to wonder if Anne really wanted to marry me or just have a wedding. We had an awful row and nearly called it all off."

Honeymoons

After the doubts and uncertainties, the excitement and fun of a wedding comes the honeymoon. Most couples recognise the need to have some time together, away from everyone. Many will go abroad. Wherever you go, even if it is only a few days by the sea, it is a valuable time to relax together.

Traditional jokes about honeymoons suggest that they are great sexual events. This is often far from the truth. *"I'd been so tense before the wedding that when we got to the airport, I was sick. And he was so hungover from his stag party, he slept all through the flight. All we wanted to do on our wedding night was sleep."*

For some couples their honeymoon will be the first time they have had a full sexual relationship. Many of those for whom sex has been part of their relationship may not have lived together. A honeymoon is not just a chance to share a bed. We come face to face with people's personal habits for the first time. This can be a real shock.

The best recipe for a successful honeymoon is to keep a sense of humour and not to expect too much:

"The first few nights were awful. We were both so tired that I just couldn't feel interested in sex. I kept thinking 'we're supposed to be having this amazing time, here we are alone'... eventually we talked about it and had a laugh and after that it was OK."

Chapter Four:
Becoming a Couple

What makes this pair a couple rather than just two individuals who live together? What adjustments have they had to make? How have they adapted to one another?

Making a home

Setting up home together is what establishes you as a couple both in the eyes of the law and society.

Where you live will depend on your work and what you can afford. Other questions you need to ask yourselves include :

– How important is the area where you live – inner city, suburb, country?

– How important is privacy, both for you as a couple and for each of you as an individual?

Answers to these kinds of questions will help you decide priorities. You may decide that living outside town is worth the cost of the fares to travel to work. On the other hand, to get a bigger flat or house you may be prepared to live in an unattractive area. Or perhaps you may decide that being central is important and that you can make do with a tiny flat.

The kind of home you create once you are through the front door poses another set of questions. Home means security for all of us but for some it is enough to have a bed and a roof overhead. For others it is somewhere to spend a lot of time together. You may agree completely on the style you want to create for yourselves or this too may be something you have to negotiate.

Choosing and creating their own home is not something every couple can afford to do. Some have to start their married life living with one pair of parents. In India the new bride automatically moves into her in-laws' home, but in the West we see setting up our own home as an important

Having your own place, somewhere to call "home", is important.

part of marriage. Even if it is just a small flat, we all like to have a place we are able to call "*home*".

"*We lived for six months with Jenny's parents. We all tried hard but I used to have rows with her Dad over daft things. I decided he was jealous of me taking away his daughter. Our sex life was awful. Jenny couldn't relax, said she was embarrassed knowing her parents were next door.*"

Living with in-laws works best if there are very business-like agreements about everything from money to cooking and cleaning, sharing facilities and privacy. It requires both partners to be sensitive. If they are your parents then your partner can easily feel an outsider in the family group. If you are with your partner's parents you need to avoid situations where your partner will feel divided loyalties between you and the family. And if the situation is difficult for you, it is no easier for parents. It may be easier to survive living in your parents' home if you know that it is only for a limited time.

Different cultures have different attitudes towards living arrangements.

Housekeeping

It can be a shock when you feel you know one another so well to discover how much there is still to know. We talk to one another about what we think and feel but our most basic beliefs about how life should be lived are something we may not even be aware of ourselves.

Most couples would probably say they believed that domestic chores should be shared especially if both partners are out at work:

*"I had stayed at Joe's flat quite often before we got married. He used to cook meals and seemed quite **domesticated**. Once we were married it all changed. He would 'help' with the washing-up, cook the odd meal and offer to get shopping on Saturdays but he just assumed that it was all my responsibility. He seemed to think I would shop and cook and clean and wash and iron for him just like his mother did. Well, my mother did it for my family so for a while I went along with it. Then one day I went mad, screamed and shouted at him, told him I hadn't got married to be his slave. I hadn't realised until then how much I was resenting it all."*

It is easy to dismiss housework as boring and unimportant but anyone saying that is usually exploiting their partner. Joe and Michelle had to take a long, hard look at their assumptions before they could decide what they felt was fair and then share out responsibilities.

There may be some real disagreements about priorities:

"I was amazed by how untidy she was. I really hated coming home every day to this chaotic flat. She said that's just how she was and she didn't think it was really important – but it was to me."

*"He seemed to have no idea about **hygiene**. He never cleaned the bath or the loo and he'd leave empty milk bottles to grow mould."*

Sorting out these kinds of issues is a matter of deciding what really

Compromises have to be made in all areas of a relationship, including housework.

matters to each of you, reaching **compromises** and agreeing who does what.

Making allowances

Becoming a couple is more than just sharing the same physical space. It is also about developing intimacy, trust and tolerance. This takes time and you may encounter difficulties on the way.

Insecurities

If we were all well-balanced, secure and confident, we would have few problems in relationships with one another. The reality is that most of us have doubts about ourselves. We can often hide them from the world outside, but in an intimate relationship it is more difficult. If we do not love ourselves, it can be difficult to believe that others find us truly lovable. The doubts can express themselves in a variety of ways:

As jealousy – *"Before we got married, I hadn't minded him seeing one of his old girlfriends from time to time, but suddenly I found I was suspicious all the time, not just about her, but girls in his office. I knew it was stupid but I couldn't help it."*

As a constant need for reassurance – *"I don't know how we survived those first few months. Jean was forever asking 'But do you really love me'. I couldn't help getting irritated and after a while I began to wonder myself."*

Fortunately the experience of loving and being loved can help to still those doubts, but it can take patience on both sides.

Privacy and independence

We all have a sense of personal space, both physical and emotional.

Privacy and personal space are necessary in any relationship.

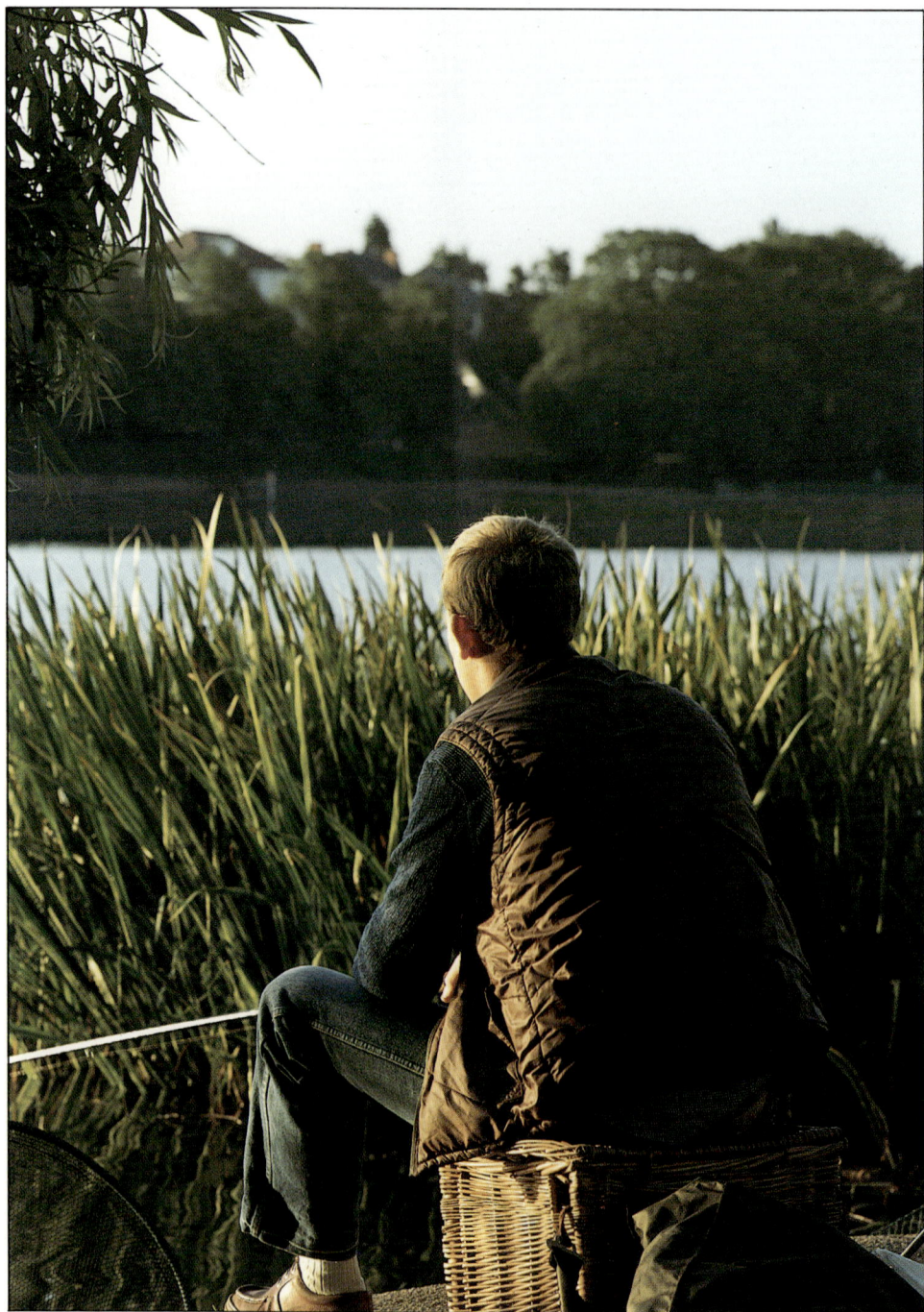

Yours may be different from your partner's.

"Anne would sometimes disappear for hours at a time to the bedroom to read a book. She said she needed to be on her own. I felt really fed up about it. It was hard for me to understand because I was used to always having people round me."

"It was obvious that Jason didn't really want me to go with him when he went off fishing. At first I really minded and nagged him about going, I suppose I thought something was wrong if we didn't do everything together. Then I decided to use the time to keep in touch with my girlfriends. Now I think it's a good thing to have some time apart. We have a great time when we are together."

Friends

By the time they marry, many couples will have friends whom they share, but each will also have some have personal friends whom their partner may not even like. It is unrealistic to expect one relationship to provide all our needs. Other friendships can strengthen a marriage as long as the couple feel secure in their own relationship. This may create problems at first:

"It was very difficult to get Ian to understand that Sandra, my best friend, was still important to me. She got on well with him, but there were times when we wanted to meet and talk on our own. He seemed to feel that if I really loved him then our relationship should be enough."

Families

However much we may criticise our own families, as soon as someone else does it we can often find ourselves passionately defending them.

Developing different interests is important for a successful relationship.

"*Debbie blew up one day when I said how mean her mother was. She went on at me about how I didn't understand what it was like for her mother and how there'd never been much money around when she was a kid so her mum had to be really careful. Yet she'd often moaned herself about how stingy her mum was.*" Because we grew up with our family's 'rules', even though we may think we have rejected them, they are still a part of us. Criticism of your partner's family feels like criticism of him or her.

You have to decide together just how involved with your own or your partner's parents you want to be. Over-involved parents can create problems:

"*My brothers and I had a fairly casual relationship with our parents. We'd pop over to see them every month or so. Ann is an only child, her mum is a widow. At first it felt like she'd moved in with us. She was always dropping round with some excuse or other, buying us things, offering to make curtains, expecting to come to lunch every Sunday. I couldn't cope with it.*"

Even when a family is not the immediate cause of a problem, their presence may be felt;

"*I didn't understand at first why Ben seemed to feel got at when I asked him about his day or what he thought about something. In our family we all talked all the time. Ben had grown up with just his Mum and spent a lot of his time trying to keep her from smothering him with attention. I realised that he was behaving the same way with me.*"

Sex

At the beginning of a relationship, sex may seem to be the most important thing about it. But after a while most couples value other things as much or more. Whenever surveys are done on the subject, the majority rate love

Talking about sex is important.

and companionship as more important than sex. When sex is good you tend to take it for granted – if it is wrong it becomes more important than anything else.

The satisfaction and excitement of sex is emotional as well as physical. Good sex is about learning how to be intimate with someone, to be able to express your needs and to be sensitive to theirs.

A satisfying relationship is one where both partners enjoy the experience. There is no one right way, just as there is no activity which is *"wrong"* as long as both partners enjoy it. Discovering what is exciting for your partner or persuading them to try something that you find exciting requires sensitivity. You also have to be able to talk about it. One of the values of reading one of the many books about the mechanics of sex is that it makes it easier to talk about it. Couples whose behaviour can be quite uninhibited under the bedclothes can be tongue-tied when it comes to talking about it.

Chapter Five:
Earning
and
Spending

Deciding how to spend money whether on big things or just the weekly shopping, can pose problems. Money means power in our society. It can also mean power in a relationship.

Sex, in-laws, and religion are delicate areas but money can be a positive minefield. In our society money is linked to power and attitudes to it often differ between men and women. Most of us grow up in households where a father clearly has the greater earning power and mother has the day-to-day responsibility, and often anxiety, of managing the **budget**. What we *think* we believe about money can sometimes be different from what we actually believe deep down. Money is the biggest cause of marital disagreements.

"*It took us ages to sort out how to organise our money. Jack said we would discuss everything, but I could see he just assumed that when it came to it, he was in charge.*"

41

"I thought Melanie was really irresponsible about money. She just refused to keep track of what she spent and just chucked bills in a drawer. We had to have a great row before I could even get her to talk about it. She said she couldn't bear to be like her mother who always had to account for every penny."

Earning

There is likely to be an imbalance in earning power between any couple. In some situations the woman may earn more but usually it is the man. In 1986 in the UK, women's weekly earnings were only 60 per cent of men's. Where there are children, it is usually the wife who takes on part-time work or loses her place in the promotion queue through taking **maternity leave**.

Joint or separate accounts?

There are a number of ways you can jointly manage your money. All earnings can be communal in a joint bank account. This will suit you if you like the idea of there being no secrets between you, and you have complete trust in one another. But it does mean that neither partner has any money that is strictly their own to do with as they please.

Alternatively, you could both retain individual accounts and a joint account into which you pay an agreed proportion of your earnings to cover the household expenses. The most important thing, whatever arrangement you chose, is that it seems fair to you both.

Budgeting

It is worth shopping around to find the kind of account in a bank or building society which meets your needs. And don't be frightened of bank managers. They need you as much as you need them. They will often give you a lot of useful, free advice.

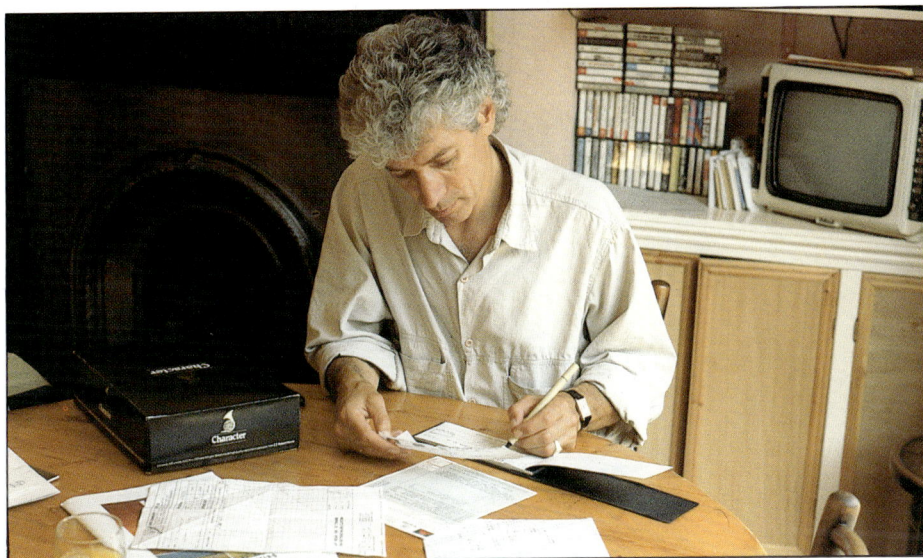

Doing the accounts.

If you have previously had a fairly casual attitude to money the idea of budgeting may seem rather boring, but to be in a perpetual state of uncertainty about your finances and forever chasing around paying final demands will mean that you spend far more time dealing with money matters than if you had sat down, planned a budget and organised paying your bills through **standing orders**.

Decisions about budgeting need to be joint ones to avoid disagreement and misunderstandings. In drawing up a budget the basics will be obvious: rent or **mortgage**, heating, food, fares etc. You may have to negotiate about whether holidays count as essentials, how much is to go on clothes, how much in savings and how much for the occasional extravagance and fun which we all need.

Saving

Whether or not you save will depend largely on your life style and priorities.

Many young couples put money aside towards buying a place of their own and towards holidays. These are very immediate needs. It may be more difficult to see the value of longer term saving but getting married is a long term commitment. **Life assurance** will, in the event of your death, prevent your partner from being left with debts to face or a large mortgage to take on. In the much more likely event of your living to get the **benefit**, it could **mature** at a time when you need money perhaps for a young family or moving house. A **savings plan** can be similarly valuable.

Retirement seems light years away, but many women are not in employer's **pension schemes**. A woman without her own pension has to rely on her husband. If she divorces, she could have only the state pension to survive on.

The big expenses

The biggest expense when you marry is setting up your own home. Renting or buying will depend on what you can afford. With a decrease in the availability of council property and high rents, especially in cities, it may be worth looking carefully to see if you can afford to buy somewhere, however small, just to get on the ownership ladder. You need to take into account though that it is not just a matter of being able to afford the mortgage – you are also responsible for maintaining the property.

Renting or buying, flat or house, you have to furnish it. We live in a society that encourages us to believe that we can have everything we want – now. Few couples can afford to buy everything at once. There are some essential items: a bed (the best quality you can afford); some comfortable chairs or a sofa or big cushions; table and chairs; cooker and fridge. After that you can economise with items from junk shops.

Essential items are a priority when furnishing your new home.

Family Planning Clinics

By appointment

Men–   Mon. Wed. Fri.
         7pm to 9pm

Women– Tues.
         7pm to 9pm

Also with
General Practitioners
upstairs (522012)

Chapter Six:
Planning a Family

Whether you want to be parking your baby's pram outside the clinic soon or in a few years time or maybe not at all, you need the best possible advice on family planning.

"*It seems strange, but we'd never really talked seriously about children before we got married. I suppose I just assumed we would one day. We were very happy together for a couple of years then Julie seemed to get really restless. She said she was fed up with her job. She also got interested in her sister's baby. She hadn't taken much notice of him before. When she said she thought it was time we had a baby I wasn't really surprised and I'd got used to the idea myself by then.*"

Julie and Ben are probably typical of many young couples in simply not being certain what they feel about a family when they marry. Time can make a lot of changes:

"*I was certain I wanted us to be just a couple. My career was really important to me and Sean went along with that but when I was 30 I suddenly felt panic-stricken at the idea I might never be a mother. I couldn't believe how strong the longing was to have a baby.*"

"*We'd always talked about how we would both like to have lots of children. Then we had Amy. I didn't enjoy the pregnancy and she's been quite a difficult baby. I don't know if I could face another, not for several years anyway.*"

Waiting a while

A couple who marry in their 30s may feel some urgency to start a family but for a young couple there is no need to rush into parenthood. Waiting two or three years before starting a family gives you time to enjoy one another and to build a secure relationship that can withstand the stresses of bringing up small children.

"*I had Michelle almost as soon as we married. It just seemed the thing to do. My Mum had me when she was very young and my sister had just had a baby. I love her a lot but I wish now we'd waited. I hadn't realised just how much time a baby took up. We can't afford to go out often so Peter and I don't really get much time together.*"

Waiting before you have children assumes that you use an efficient method of **contraception**. Finding the method that suits both of you is a matter of going to a **family planning** clinic or your GP. No method is perfect. The **pill** is the most reliable but used long term carries health risks. Mechanical methods such as the **cap**, **condoms** or **IUD** carry fewer risks but can be less reliable. The **rhythm method** may be the only acceptable method to Catholics. You need to get as much information as possible

Planning a family is a major decision.

Seek advice at your local family planning clinic.

about all the methods available, and then choose the method that suits you as a couple.

Ready for children?

The first question to ask yourselves is do you really want children? This may not be the same as wanting a baby. The urge to have a baby can be very strong, especially in women. But the longed-for adorable bundle will grow into a determined toddler, a gangly school-child, a rebellious adolescent.

Having a baby is something we do to please ourselves. But once the baby arrives it is a person with rights and needs. You need to be sure you are ready to take these on and to ask yourselves some serious questions. *"It's always seemed unfair that people who want to adopt are so carefully vetted, while some couples conceive babies without any thought at all. It's tough on the babies."*

50

Are you ready to share your life with another person?

Having a baby, however longed-for, changes your relationship as a couple. You have someone else to consider as well as each other. Caring for a baby can be exhausting and creates stresses. Parents may both love the baby but this in itself can cause jealousy especially for a new father who has been used to his wife's exclusive attention. Suddenly he finds he has to compete with this demanding small person with whom she is so obviously and deeply in love.

What about money?

After the initial expenses of pram, cot, baby clothes, a tiny baby does not make many financial demands. But children become ever more expensive as they grow older. And having a baby means that one of you, usually the mother, will have to give up working to look after him or her, or else employ a childminder. Either way you will have a cut in income.

Are you fit enough to have a baby?

If you are both fit and well and eating healthily at the time of conception, this gives a baby the best possible start in life. It will also help the mother through pregnancy and both of you through the tiring early months of caring for a tiny baby.

The wrong reasons

The only reason for having a baby is because you both want children. There are some reasons which may seem convincing but are not really about wanting children and can lead to a lot of unhappiness:

Patching up a shaky relationship

It can be easy to fool yourselves that a baby will bring you together. It can certainly do so in a basically secure relationship. In a relationship already under stress it is more likely to be the last straw.

Giving a purpose to life

A young woman who lacks confidence in her abilities can feel that having a baby will fill the void. Perhaps it will for a few years but eventually children grow up and the dissatisfaction will still be there. Having a baby is not an alternative to finding out what you really want from life.

Everyone expects it

Parents and in-laws keep dropping hints, friends all have children, even younger brothers and sisters have children. This can be a real pressure on a couple to conform. But the decision to have children must be your own.

One partner wants a baby

A wife who does not really want a baby may be transformed into a doting mother once the baby arrives. Similarly, the wife who knows her husband does not want a baby but deliberately gets pregnant may find she has a baby but loses a husband. In neither is there any thought as to the needs of the baby.

Choice *vs* chance

Whether you want a big family or just one child, whether you want to be parents while you are young and energetic or wait until you are older and more experienced are decisions you will need to make together. We quite rightly expect to make decisions and take control over something as important as having children. We tend to talk about 'family planning' and assume we can control everything about it.

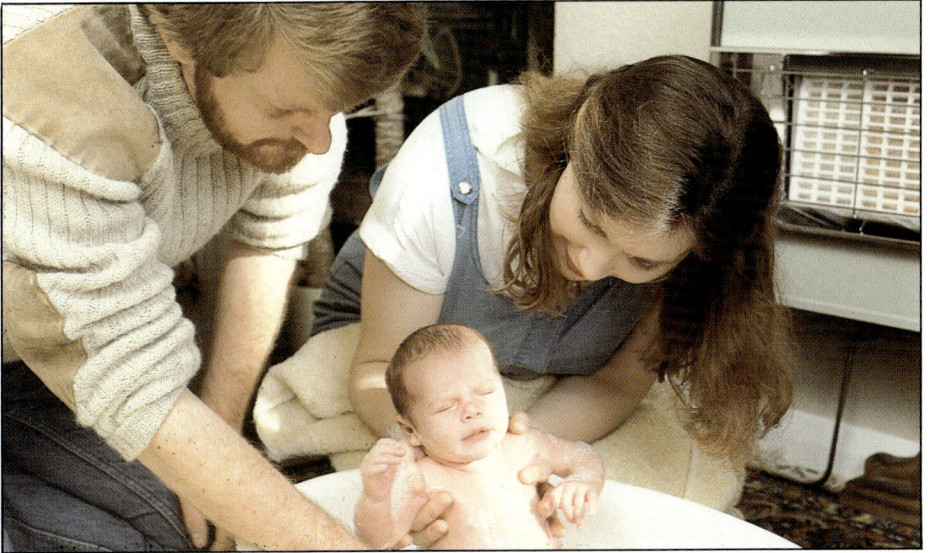

Babies involve a lot of responsibility for the whole family.

Not all pregnancies are planned. We do not plan to be infertile, or to have a **miscarriage** or a handicapped baby. We do not plan to have a baby who never sleeps, a **hyperactive** toddler or a teenager who takes drugs. Nor do we plan to be ill, unemployed, divorced or bereaved. But these things happen and can upset all our careful planning. Being flexible, coping with change and making the best of things are important qualities in parents.

Chapter Seven:
Problem Solving

Are their problems bringing them together, helping them to a better understanding of one another and a closer relationship? Or are they driving them apart? If so this couple needs help.

Everyone has problems, everyone has arguments. It can be much healthier to have a good row than to continually nag at each other, or to bottle it up. Anger which you keep to yourself does not simply go away. It is either stored up as resentment, or it is turned in against yourself and becomes depression, headaches or illness.

Constructive arguments

Saying everything you need to say even if you do get upset and shout can clear the air and at the end of it you will make up and feel closer than before.

"*But I am a really easy-going person, I never get angry.*" Are you sure? Or did you perhaps grow up in a family where anger was not allowed? Or maybe there was violence between your parents, so anger feels a really dangerous thing? If you cannot express what you feel because you are afraid of your partner, then your relationship is not an equal one and you may need to seek help in learning to change this.

Arguments are healthy only if they are constructive, that is, at the end of them there is a sense of release and you both understand one another better. This is more likely to happen if you:

– Talk about whatever upsets you at the time it happens – not in the middle of the party – but as soon as you get home. If you don't, the whole

Arguments can be constructive if they resolve something.

thing can build up out of proportion as you brood over it resentfully.

– Come right out with it. Don't sulk in order to gain attention, or leave your partner to guess what is wrong. This will lead to a feeling of resentment which will make talking about things even more difficult.

– Talk about your own feelings. "*I feel really upset when you laugh at me in public*", not, "*You're always upsetting me...*". If you accuse your partner, naturally they will be defensive and less likely to listen to you.

– Identify the real problem. It is easier to nag about the mess your partner makes in the bathroom than to say that you are worried because you don't seem to be making love very often, but this will not solve the problem.

– Ask your partner to discuss a problem with you. Don't nag about it. Nagging is always unproductive since you simply repeat the same complaints without any real discussion and the situation stays just the same.

– Ask yourself whether the thing that is a problem for you can be changed:

"*Soon after we married, Paul had a spell of working late several evenings a week. I felt I hardly seemed to see him. I used to moan about it but when I talked to my mum she pointed out he was doing it to build up the business for both of us and it would get better. I realised it was pointless minding about it and I started going to an evening class. I really enjoyed it and we got on better after that.*"

– Learn to listen. It is easy to be so caught up in our own feelings we do not listen properly. Your partner wants to be heard and understood just as much as you do. Sometimes a row is just about wanting to be listened to and understood. Sometimes it is about something that needs one or both of you to change.

Getting help

Constructive rows sound all very fine on paper. With honesty and determination most problems can be solved. But what happens when you get stuck in a cycle of arguments you can't seem to break? What if you realise that the feelings involved are too upsetting, too deep-rooted for you to deal with on your own? A friend or someone in the family may be the person to talk to, but they may feel too involved themselves not to take sides. You may be able to get help from someone you respect, such as a sympathetic family doctor or church minister.

If none of these can help, you need to seek counselling. Your doctor or Citizens Advice Bureau will be able to tell you what is available locally either free or at a modest fee. There is nothing shameful in seeking help, on the contrary it is a responsible and creative step. Living in a miserable situation simply takes away your energy and self-confidence.

Counselling

You need to decide whether one or both of you wants individual

Marriage guidance may provide a solution.

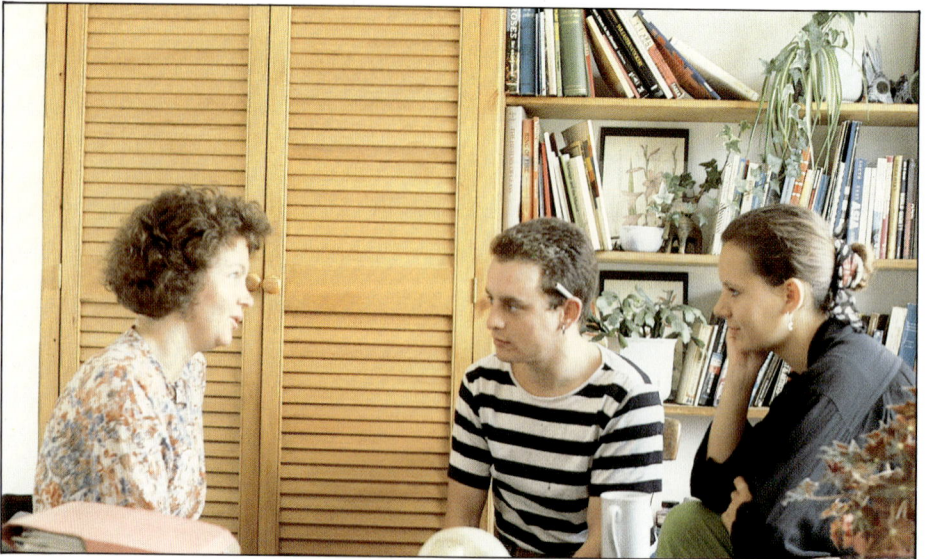

counselling, or whether you want to go together. There are a variety of agencies who may be able to help. In most parts of the UK, Relate (previously the Marriage Guidance Council) will have a branch. They may have quite a long waiting list, so don't wait until things are so bad that you are no longer talking to each other.

A counsellor can only help you if you want to help yourselves. Counselling cannot transform your relationship overnight. It can help you to see what your problems really are and help you discover new ways of dealing with them. If you both care enough about your relationship you will be able to use it to go on to create a better and stronger marriage.

Glossary

Abortion – the death of a foetus before 20 weeks from the last period or before the foetus weighs a little over a pound.

Alcoholism – the action of alcohol upon the human system; diseased condition produced by it.

Assets – properties or effects.

Budget – to plan expenditure according to financial resources.

Cap – a round dome of thin rubber which can be placed in the girl's vagina before sex to help prevent pregnancy.

Chaperon – a person who accompanies a young unmarried woman in public, as guide and protector.

Compromise – settlement of an argument by concession on both sides.

Condom – a tube of thin rubber, closed at one end, which can be rolled down over the boy's penis before sex. Helps prevent pregnancy and protects against sexually transmitted diseases.

Contraception – devices used to prevent pregnancy when you have sex.

Dependent – a person who depends on another for support.

Divorce – the legal dissolution of a marriage.

Domesticate – to be involved in the home and its responsibilities.

Family planning clinic – clinic which gives help and advice about contraception and pregnancy to young people.

Fertility – the ability to become pregnant (for a girl), or the ability to make a girl pregnant (for a boy).

Hygiene – a system or routine which is necessary for health.

Hyperactive – excessive energy in children, can be a nervous reaction to too many preservatives in the diet.

Intrauterine device (IUD) – a small plastic birth control device which can be inserted into a woman's uterus to prevent pregnancy.

Legal rights – a person's entitlements, according to the law.

Life assurance – the action of securing the payment of a specified sum in the event of a person's death.

Maternity leave – period of absence from work, often paid, to allow a pregnant woman to prepare for the birth of her child.

Mature – in legal terms, the time at which a policy or pension becomes due for payment.

Mortgage – a financial loan, agreed by the bank or building society, which is used towards the purchase of property.

Norm – an accepted standard.

Pill – a method of birth control which copies the cycle of hormones in order to prevent pregnancy.

Pros and cons – the advantages and disadvantages of a situation.

Psychological – a process concerned with the mind.

Pension scheme – a scheme into which money is paid in order to ensure that a person is provided for in old age. These schemes can either be privately organised, or state-run.

Racism – prejudice against colour.

Relationship – a state of friendship or familiarity between two people.

Retirement – the end of a person's working life.

Rhythm method – a method of birth control based on abstaining (not having sex) on certain days.

Ritual – a tradition or rite practised in society.

Savings plan – a scheme for encouraging the saving of money.

Sexual equality – a system which encourages equal opportunities for both men and women.

Wooing – courtship

Index

Photographic credits

Cover: Vanessa Bailey; pages 4, 6, 8, 11, 18, 28, 31, 46, 53 and 54: J. Allan Cash Photo Library; pages 7, 14, 19 and 48: Magnum Photos; page 10: Shaun Barlow; page 12: Anthea Sieveking/Network; pages 16, 21, 30, 35, 39, 40, 43, 44, 56, 58: Marie-Helene Bradley; page 22: Roger Vlitos; page 24: Barry Lewis/Network; pages 26, 36 and 50: Robert Harding Photo Library; page 33: Flick Killerby.